MW01073461

Therapy Cracks Me Up!

Therapy Cracks Me Up!

Jean Rosenfeld, LCSW

Printed in the United States of America

Cover and Interior Design: Vanessa Perez
vlperez@sbcglobal.net

First Printing, 2017

ISBN-13 978-1544748894
ISBN-10 1544748892

Jeanrosenfeld@gmail.com
Carmichael, California

ACKNOWLEDGMENTS

Much gratitude goes to my husband, George Rosenfeld—you have been a source of support and inspiration as I've cartooned my way through most of our 50+ year relationship. Your critiquing and tweaking have been invaluable. To Stephanie Kurek, I am grateful for your encouragement and "Mom just do it!" attitude along with your practical hurdle help that moved me along the path to creating this book. And to Sunny Lerner, thank you for your cheerleading all along the way.

Thank you to graphic artist, Vanessa Perez, for the cover design and book formatting. Your talent and expertise have been invaluable. I am grateful to Shauna Smith for your years of inspiration and prodding, and to Susheel Bibbs for your advice and spurring me on. Special thanks go to Ruth Ross for her book design ideas (Check out www.ruthrossart.com). And much love and appreciation go to my brother, David Aaronson, and my dear circle of friends who have assessed and commented on the cartoons and boosted my confidence.

One last thank you goes to my mother, May Aaronson, who raised me to a chorus of, "You should publish that!"

FROM THE CARTOONIST

I often feel the urge to comment in comic form as I watch the impact on psychotherapy of ever-changing therapeutic modalities, diagnoses and medications. My cartoons also reflect the influence on our daily lives of rapidly changing political, social and cultural forces.

These cartoons have been published in *The Therapist,* the bi-monthly magazine of the California Association of Marriage and Family Therapists, and the newsletters for both the California Society for Clinical Social Work and the Clinical Social Work Association, as well as various websites.

I hope you enjoy them!

TABLE OF CONTENTS

Imaginings and Insights...........................13

Happy Hour – Depressed Hour 14
Stem Cell Identity Crisis 15
Cupid 16
Men Are from Cars 17
Jack Has Agoraphobia 18
Potato Head Gender Identity 19
Mental Health Pyramid..............20
Poverty Barn..............21
Workaholics Anonymous..............22
Personal Remote Controller 23
$Megacorp$ on the Couch..............24
New Brain Structures 25
F*ck-it List 26
Statue of Liberty 27

Relationships...........................29

Couple on Cell Phones 30
Powerpoint Presentation 31
Pre-emptive Strike 32
Mindful Breathing, Eating, Walking 33
Self-Observant or Self-Absorbed? 34
Honk If You Think… 35
Yelling Until You Love Me 36
Fake News 37

Kids..39

Favorite Laptop 40
American Dream Analysis 41
Shrink Problems So They Don't Fit 42
Slinky...43
Attention Deficit Disorder 44
Art of Reframing 45
Five Day Family Forecast 46
Facebook – Electronic Superego Enhancer 47
No App for Navigating Life 48
American Idle..49

Women..51

Insights Are Closer 52
Childhood Pre-Existing Condition 53
Email, Facebook 54
Parentectomy 55
Happy Face Leaves Therapy 56
Shoes..57
Extreme Personality Makeover 58
Sugar and Spice 59
Anorexia 60
Botox 61
Memory Like Voting Machines 62

Men 63

His Brain Has Mind of Its Own 64
Post Truth Stress Disorder 65
My Inner Child...66
Reality TV – Nymphomaniac 67
Worry Surfing...68
My Lawyer Within....................................69
Posttraumatic Taxes Disorder 70
False Memory Syndrome..........................71

Therapists...73

Will Empathize for Food 74
Creative Marketing 75
Trump University...................................76
How's My Empathy? 77
A Difficult Diagnosis 78
Siri Is Now a Therapist 79
Diagnostic Decision Trees 80
Had Enough! Brief Therapy....................81
Your Hour Is Up....................................82
Diagnosis by Daisy Petal Picking 83
Beam Me Up 84
Why Come to Therapy? 85
DSM 5 Workshop 86
Personal Trainer 87
Self-Help for Therapist Burnout 88
Psychotherapy Dumbed Down 89
Medication Help or Hurt? 90
Heart in Hand 91
Compulsive Spending 92
Daydreams of a Therapist 93
Next Therapist 200 Miles.......................94

Animals..95

Cat Video 96
Polar – Not Bipolar................................97
Elephant in the Room 98
Balloon Animals 99
Fly Trauma Center 100

Imaginings and Insights

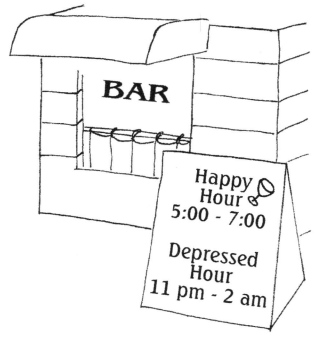

Happy Hour
5:00 - 7:00

Depressed Hour
11 pm - 2 am

©2016 Jean Rosenfeld

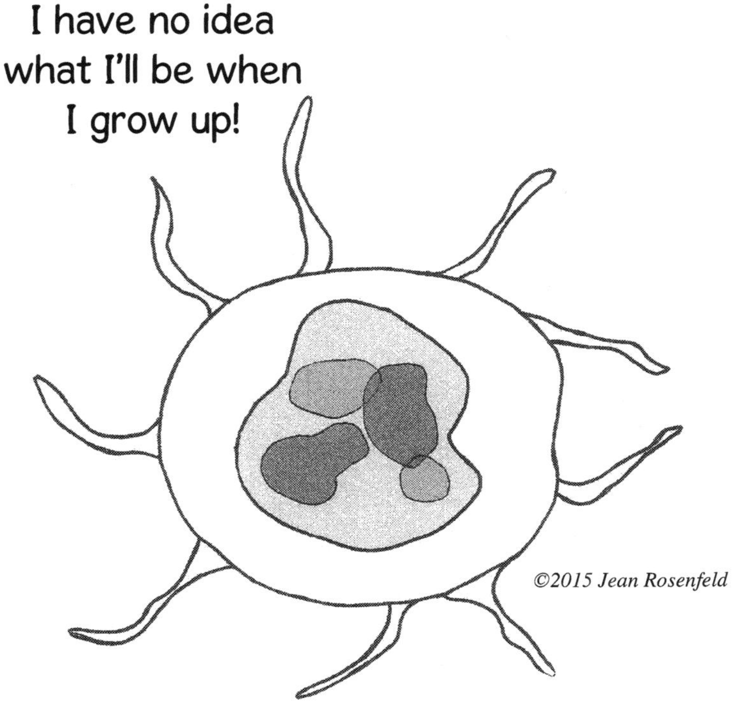
I have no idea what I'll be when I grow up!
©2015 Jean Rosenfeld

Clem the Stem Cell has an identity crisis.

OK – from now on I promise to check for compatibility. But you won't have as many clients!

©2006 Jean Rosenfeld

MEN ARE
FROM CARS
Women Are
from Kleenex

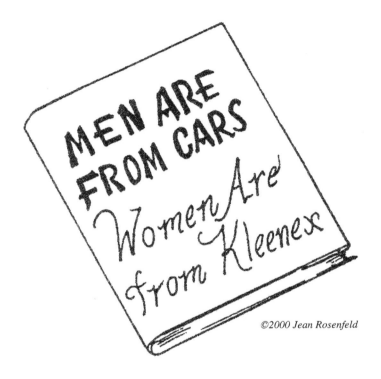

©2000 Jean Rosenfeld

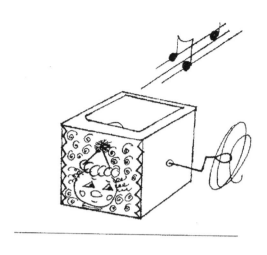

©1998 Jean Rosenfeld

Jack has developed
agoraphobia

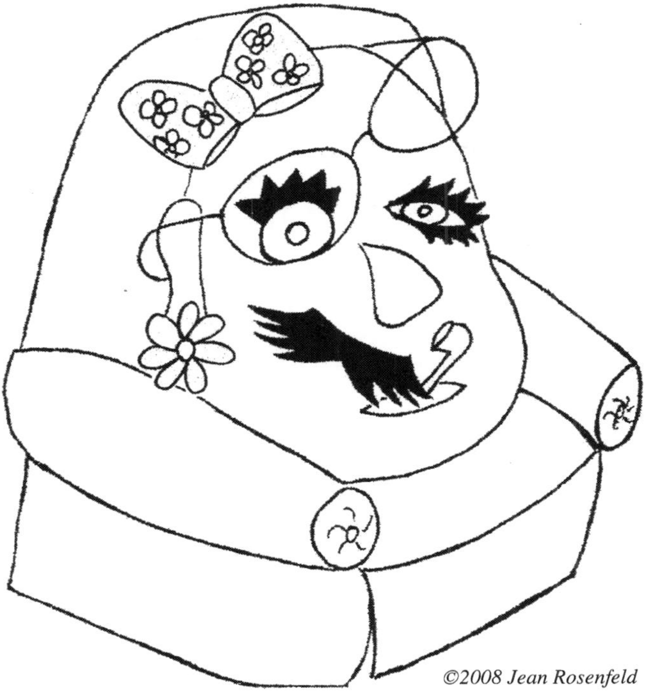
©2008 Jean Rosenfeld

Potato Head experiments with
gender identity.

HAPPINESS

EXERCISE

LOVE / WORK \ PLAY

©2014 Jean Rosenfeld

MENTAL HEALTH PYRAMID

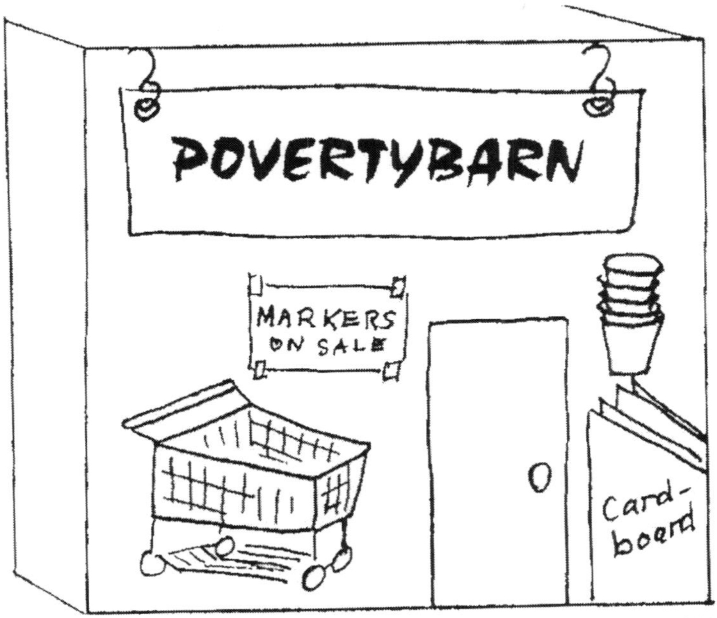
POVERTYBARN
MARKERS ON SALE
Card-board

©2008 Jean Rosenfeld

Your next stop after Home Repo

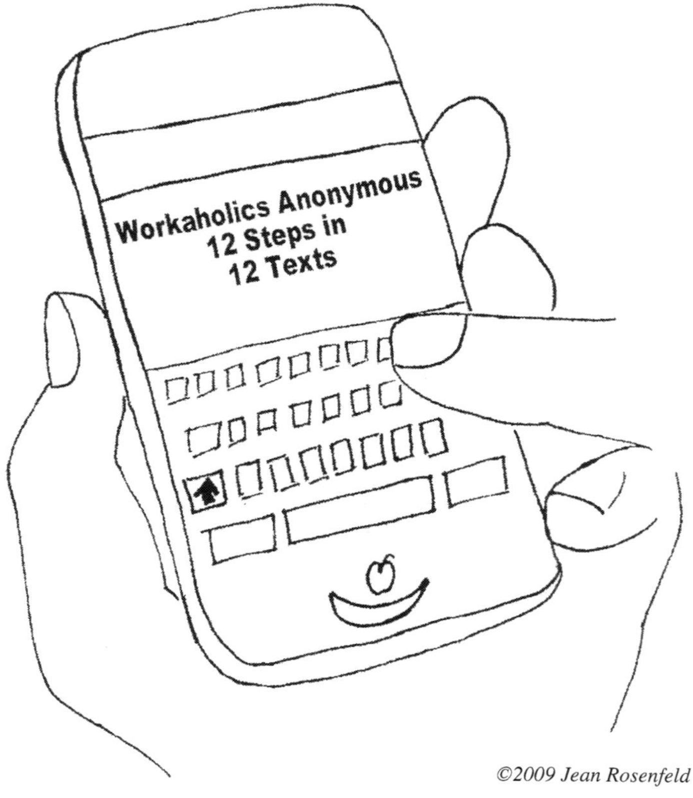
Workaholics Anonymous
12 Steps in
12 Texts

Personal
Remote
Controller
MUTE
INTROVERTER
EXTROVERTER
ENERGY
EMOTIONS
EMPATHY
SOCIO-
PATHY
CO-
DEPENDENCE
BOUNDARIES
SLEEP
REALITY

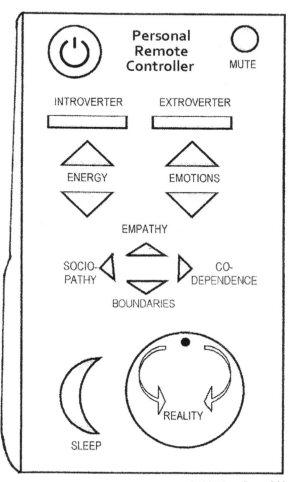

©1991 Jean Rosenfeld

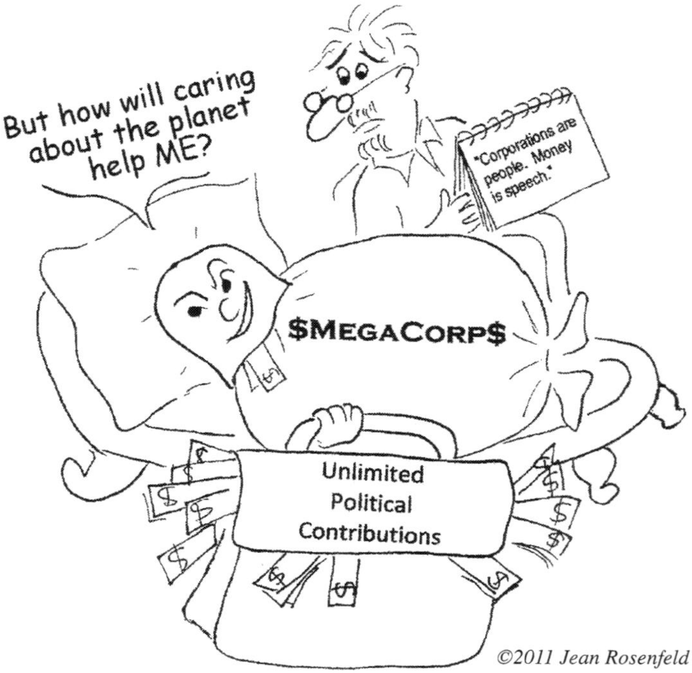
But how will caring about the planet help ME?
"Corporations are people. Money is speech."
$MEGACORP$
Unlimited Political Contributions
©2011 Jean Rosenfeld

MRI Reveals New Structures in The Brain

BIPOLAR REGION
ABANDONED MIND
STATE OF DENIAL
GENERATION GAP
RANGE OF AFFECT
TOWER OF STRENGTH
PEAK EXPERIENCE
VALLEY OF DEPRESSION
MOUNTAIN OF SHAME
ISLAND OF NORMALITY
HEIGHT OF CONFUSION
COMMUNICATION GULF
ROCK OF STABILITY
VOLCANO OF RAGE
SELF-ESTEEM FALLS
SEA OF TRANQUILLITY
STATE OF EUPHORIA
CROSS ROADS OF LIFE
FANTASY ISLAND
WAVES OF ANXIETY

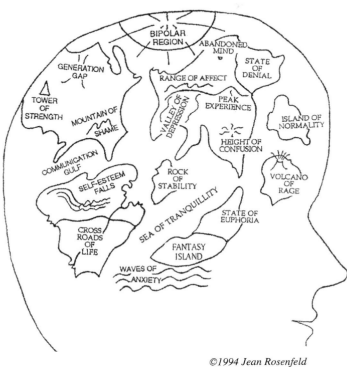

©1994 Jean Rosenfeld

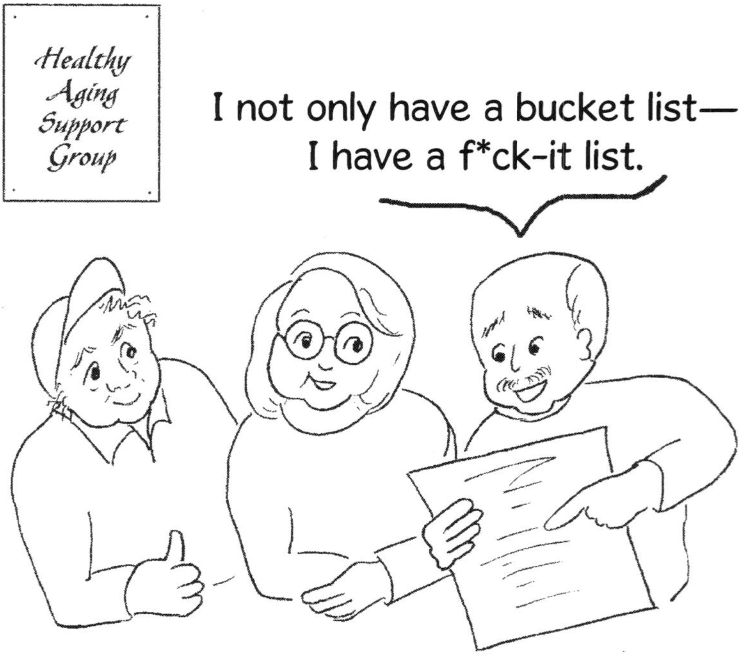
Healthy
Aging
Support
Group
I not only have a bucket list—
I have a f*ck-it list.

"You're Fired!"

©2017 Jean Rosenfeld

Relationships

©2015 Jean Rosenfeld

Instead of TELLING you
about my wife's faults,
I've prepared a
POWERPOINT presentation.

©2008 Jean Rosenfeld

I didn't start the fight—
That was a pre-emptive strike!

©1990 Jean Rosenfeld

Mindful breathing...
Mindful eating...
Mindful walking...

He's so mindful
he doesn't hear
a word I say!

©2009 Jean Rosenfeld

My therapist says
I'm very self-observant,
that's why I take so
many selfies.

Self-observant
or
self-absorbed?

©2016 Jean Rosenfeld

Honk if you think my husband drinks too much.
Honk if you think my wife needs therapy.

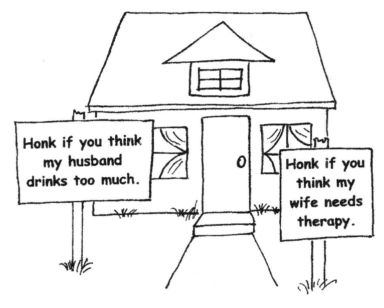

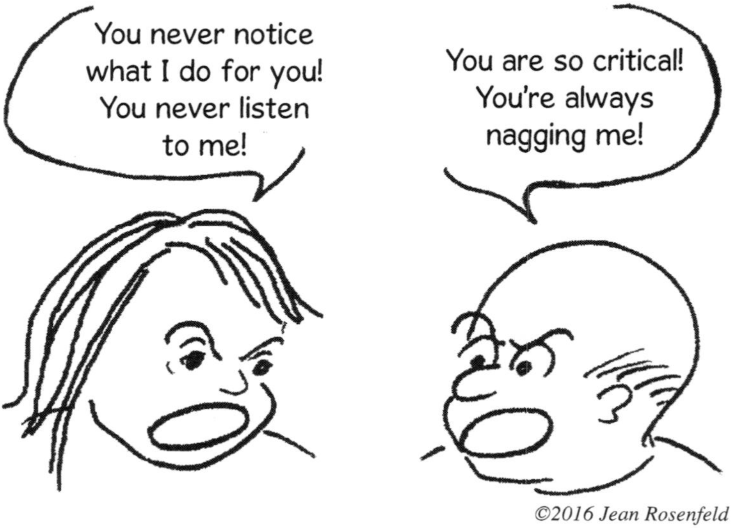
You never notice what I do for you! You never listen to me!
You are so critical! You're always nagging me!
©2016 Jean Rosenfeld

The "I'm going to yell at you until you love me," approach to marriage.

I don't believe any
of your excuses.
They are all fake news!

©2017 Jean Rosenfeld

Kids

I thought
I was your
favorite
laptop.

©1998 Jean Rosenfeld

I'm tired of being LOVABLE.
I want to be THIN and BLONDE like Barbie,
with lots of CLOTHES and ACCESSORIES.

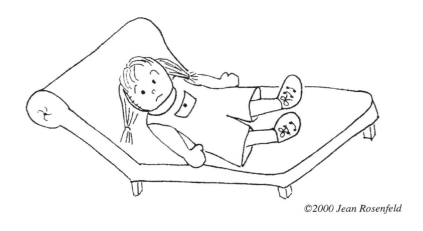

©2000 Jean Rosenfeld

American Dream Analysis

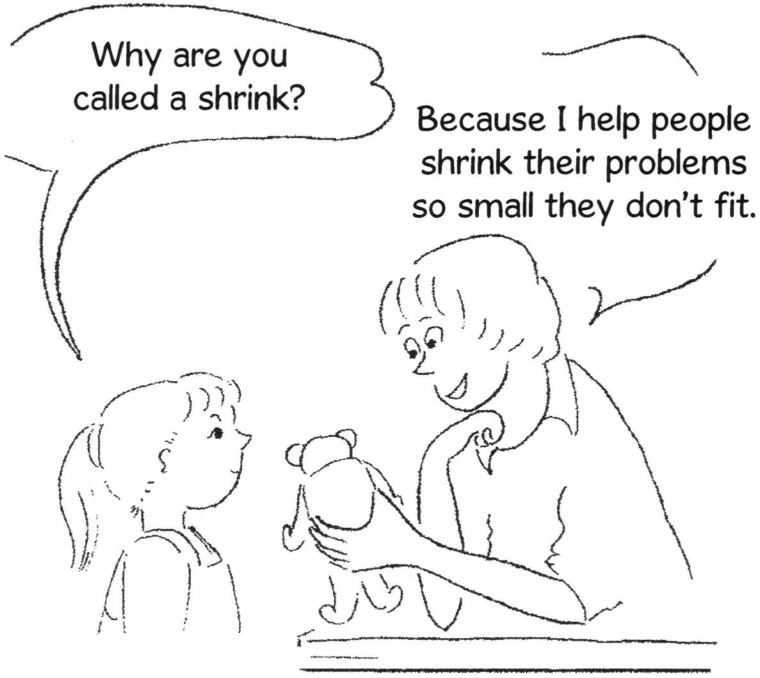
Why are you called a shrink?
Because I help people shrink their problems so small they don't fit.

The first step
is always the hardest.

©1996 Jean Rosenfeld

I have
Attention
Deficit
Disorder.
I need more
ATTENTION!!

©1996 Jean Rosenfeld

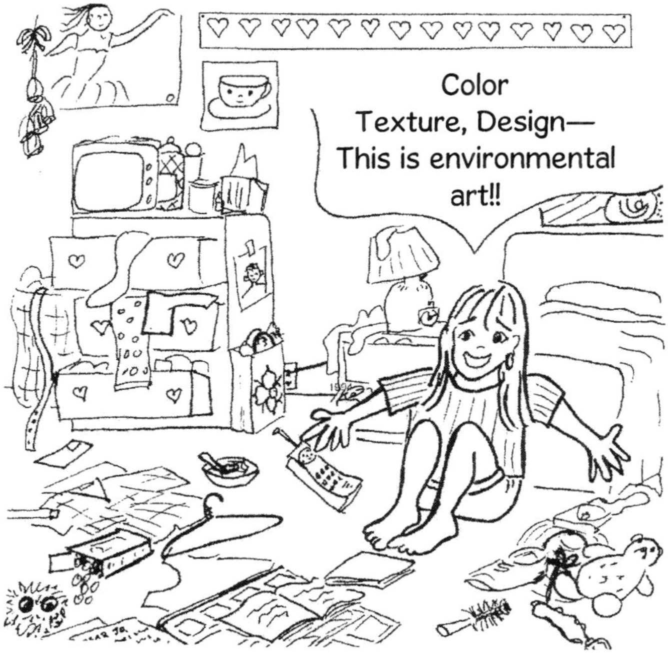
Color Texture, Design— This is environmental art!!

The fine art of reframing

Five Day Family Forecast
Cold front approcahing with frosty stares and stormy outbursts.
Followed by sunshine and smiles.
A high pressure system will come in for the weekend.
With temperaments predominantly in the teens.
Low lying fog and confusion will lift with a 60% chance of warmth and affection.

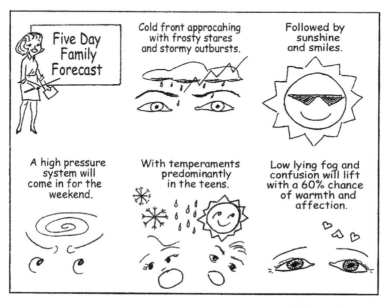

©1994 Jean Rosenfeld

I was partying and got really drunk and someone posted video of me on Facebook!!! I can't do anything anymore!

Hmmm... Facebook, The Electronic Superego Enhancer.

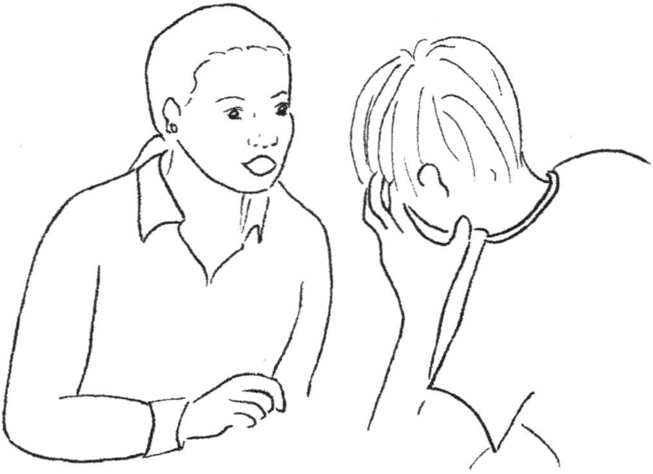

©2013 Jean Rosenfeld

No—There's no app for navigating your life.
But you did come fully loaded with a brain
and a heart to help you find your way.

My parents want me to work harder in school, but I'm an American Idle.

©1994 Jean Rosenfeld

Women

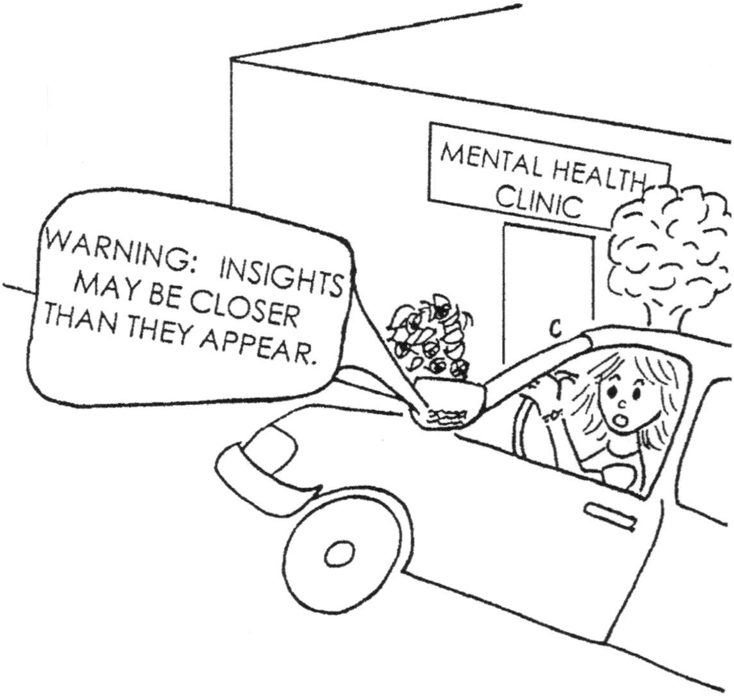
MENTAL HEALTH CLINIC
C
WARNING: INSIGHTS MAY BE CLOSER THAN THEY APPEAR.

Does having had a
childhood count
as a pre-existing
condition?

©1996 Jean Rosenfeld

I email.
I facebook.
I snapchat.
I text.
I tweet...
Sorry,
I have no time
for a
relationship.

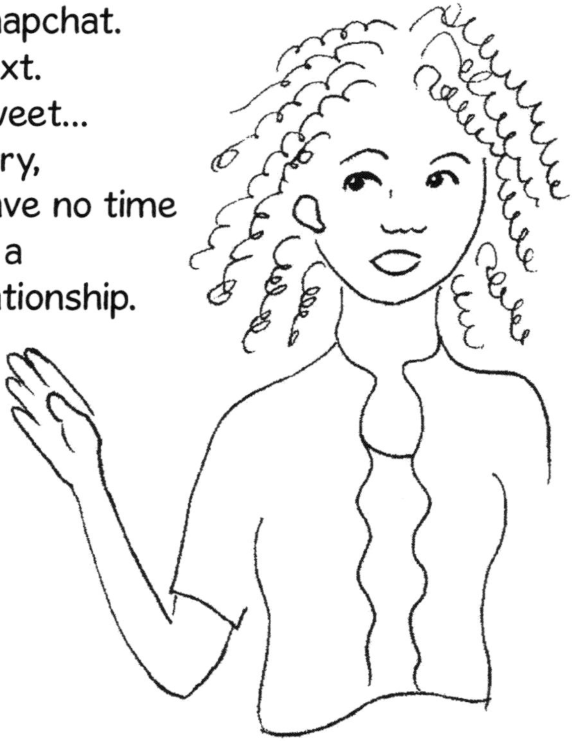

Sometimes
a parentectomy
is needed.

©2009 Jean Rosenfeld

I'm ready to leave therapy now.

Shoes can make
or break an
outfit.

Shoes can make
or break an
ankle!

Proposed Diagnosis: **DisShoeLexia,** an enduring pattern
of wearing shoes that are painful and damaging to the body.

This disorder is not related to **DisShoeLacia,** the inability to
tie shoes so they stay tied.

©2008 Jean Rosenfeld

I'm looking for a therapist

who does

Extreme

Personality

Makeovers!!

©1994 Jean Rosenfeld

Sugar and spice
and everything nice,
that's what Codependents
are made of.

The look to die for—
Anorexia

©2008 Jean Rosenfeld

Faster than psychotherapy

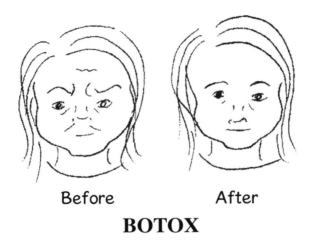

Before   After

BOTOX

©1999 Jean Rosenfeld

My memory
is like those
Voting Machines.
If I don't have
a paper trail -
I can't trust it.

©2004 Jean Rosenfeld

Men

His brain has
a mind of its own.

©2003 Jean Rosenfeld

I have PTSD—
Post Truth Stress Disorder

©2017 Jean Rosenfeld

My inner child
can beat your
inner
child!

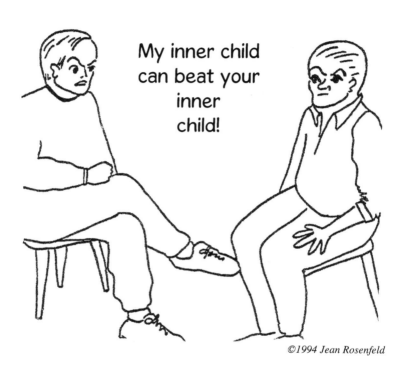

Reality TV—My favorite
escape from reality.

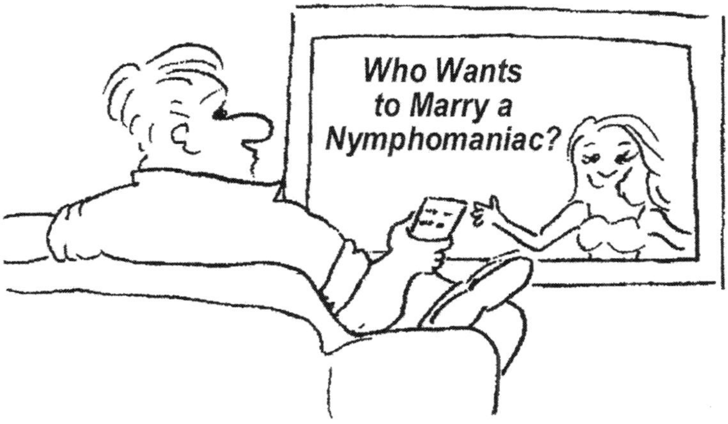
Who Wants
to Marry a
Nymphomaniac?

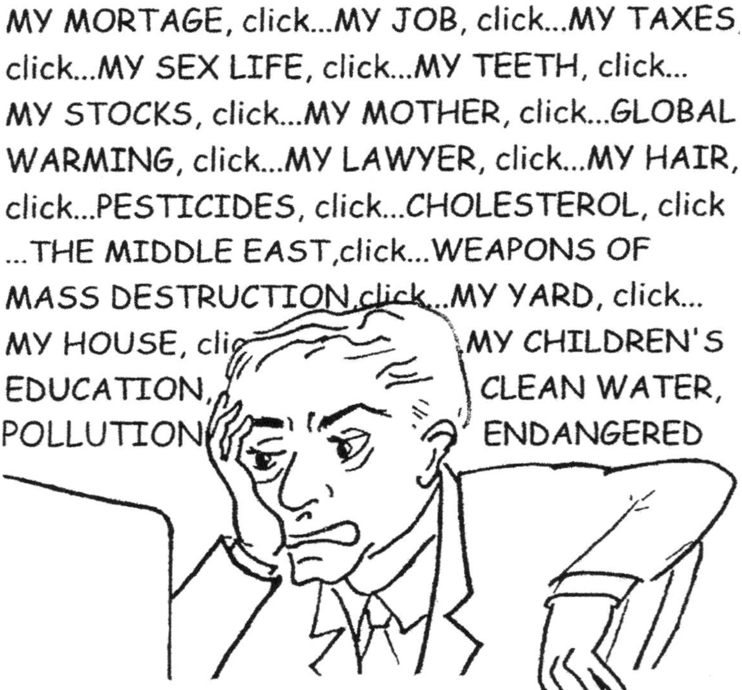
MY MORTAGE, click...MY JOB, click...MY TAXES
click...MY SEX LIFE, click...MY TEETH, click...
MY STOCKS, click...MY MOTHER, click...GLOBAL
WARMING, click...MY LAWYER, click...MY HAIR,
click...PESTICIDES, click...CHOLESTEROL, click
...THE MIDDLE EAST,click...WEAPONS OF
MASS DESTRUCTION,click...MY YARD, click...
MY HOUSE, cli
MY CHILDREN'S
EDUCATION,
CLEAN WATER,
POLLUTION
ENDANGERED

WORRY SURFING

©2009 Jean Rosenfeld

©1994 Jean Rosenfeld

My lawyer within wants to sue
my parents without.

APRIL 16th

My clients have a Seasonal Affective problem that happens every spring –

Posttraumatic Taxes Disorder.

(I think I have it too.)

False Memory Syndrome

©1994 Jean Rosenfeld

Therapists

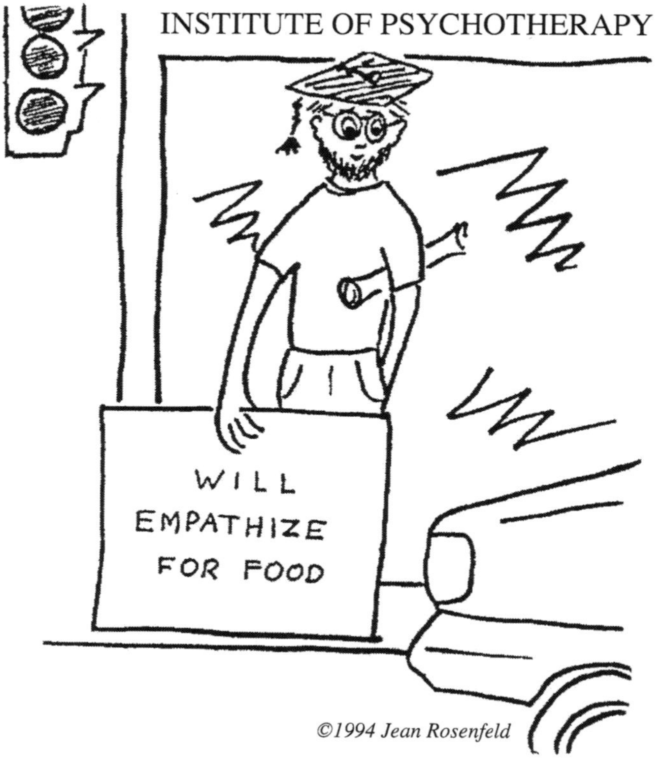
INSTITUTE OF PSYCHOTHERAPY
WILL
EMPATHIZE
FOR FOOD

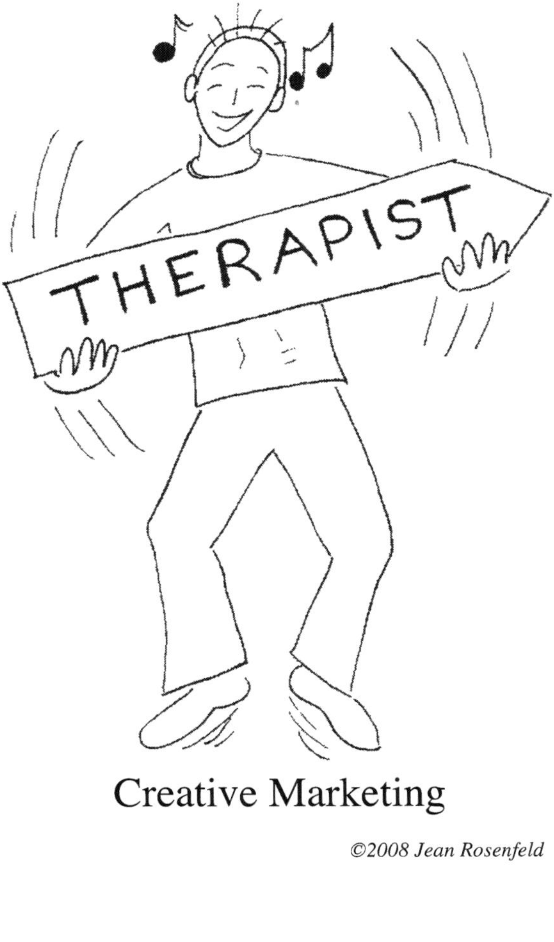
THERAPIST

Creative Marketing

©2008 Jean Rosenfeld

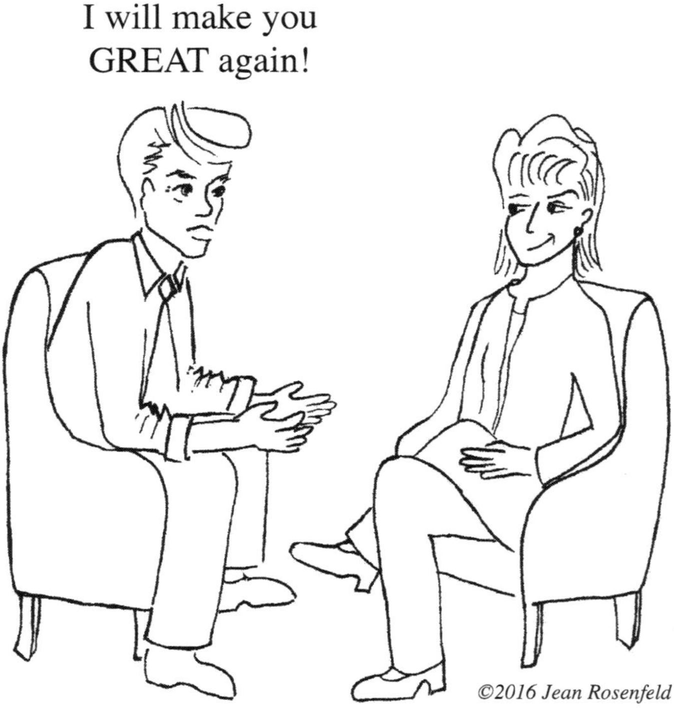
I will make you GREAT again!
©2016 Jean Rosenfeld

Trump University—School of Psyhotherapy

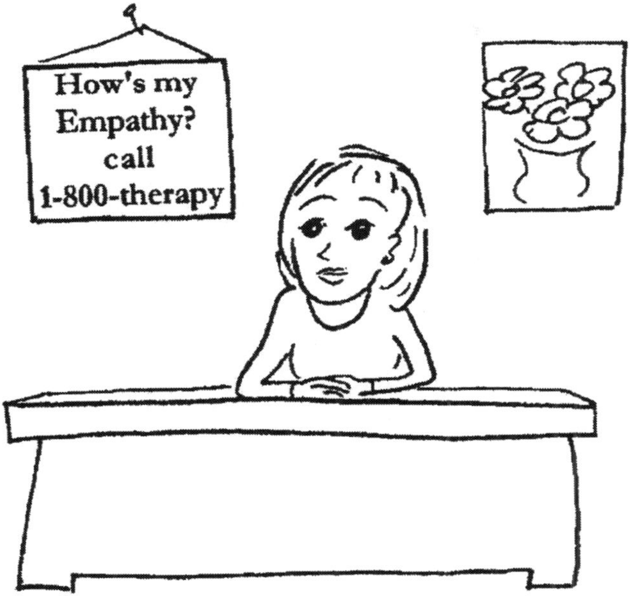
How's my
Empathy?
call
1-800-therapy

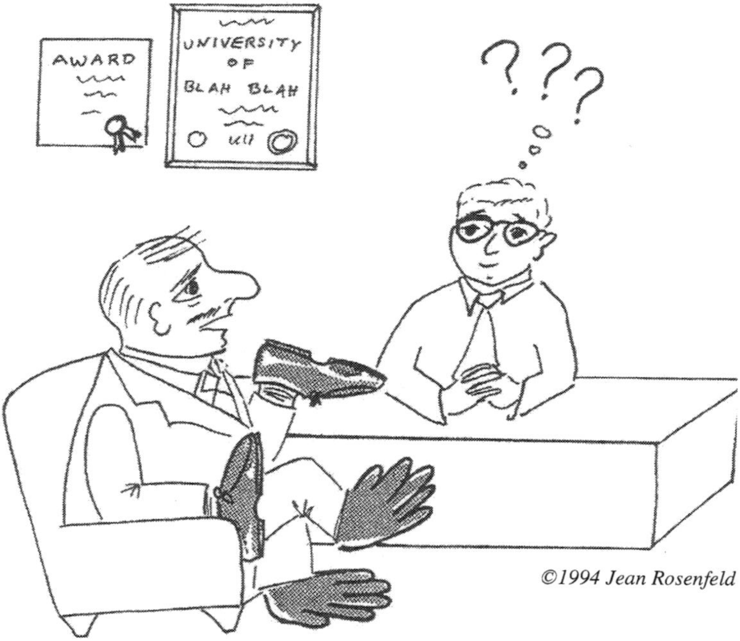
AWARD
UNIVERSITY OF BLAH BLAH
©1994 Jean Rosenfeld

Sometimes diagnosis is difficult.

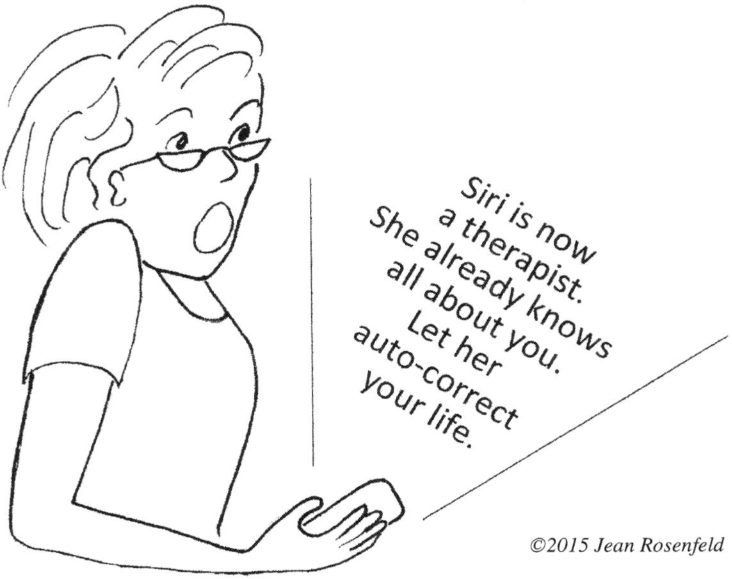
Siri is now
a therapist.
She already knows
all about you.
Let her
auto-correct
your life.

©2015 Jean Rosenfeld

DIAGNOSTIC DECISION TREES

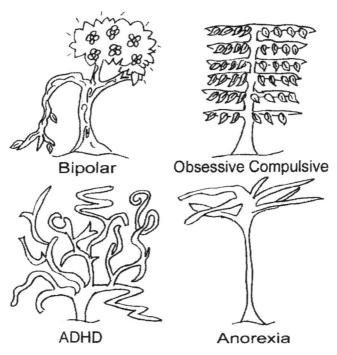

Bipolar

Obsessive Compulsive

ADHD

Anorexia

©2014 Jean Rosenfeld

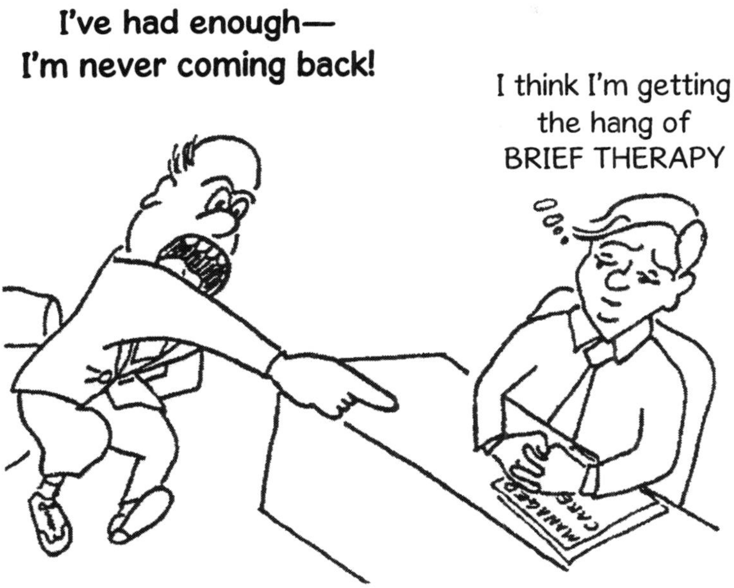
I've had enough—
I'm never coming back!
I think I'm getting
the hang of
BRIEF THERAPY

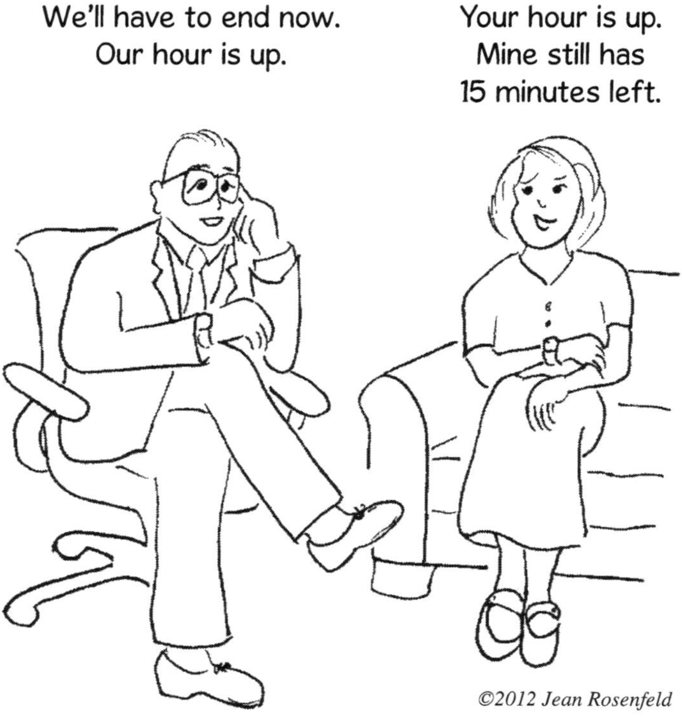
We'll have to end now. Our hour is up.
Your hour is up. Mine still has 15 minutes left.
©2012 Jean Rosenfeld

DIANOSIS BY DAISY PETAL PICKING

NARCISSISTIC

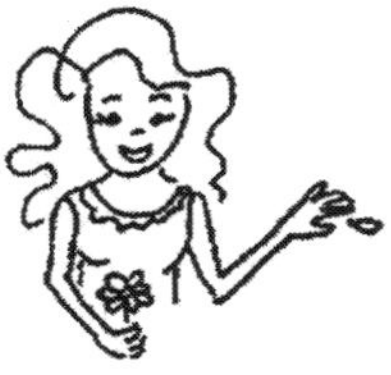

THEY ALL LOVE ME...
THEY ALL LOVE ME NOT.

ATTENTION DEFICIT DISORDER

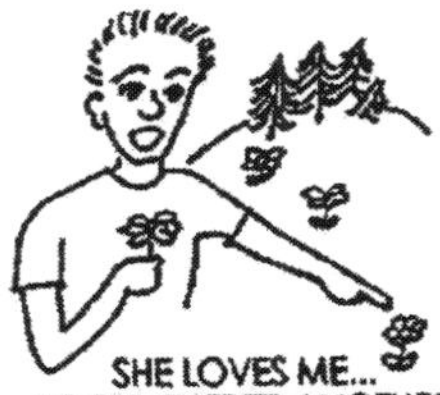

SHE LOVES ME...
LOOK! THERE'S ANOTHER
DAISY OVER THERE!

DEPENDENT

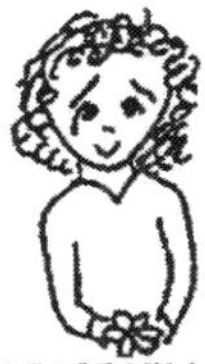

I PLEASE HIM...
I PLEASE HIM NOT.

BORDERLINE

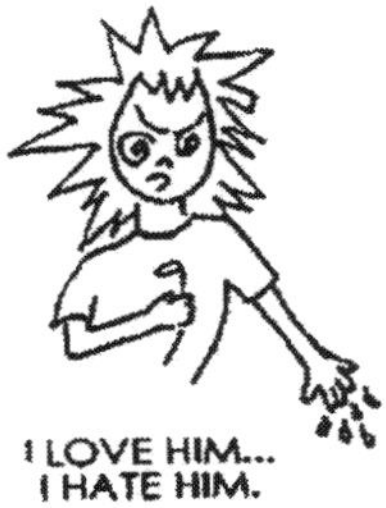

I LOVE HIM...
I HATE HIM.

PARANOID

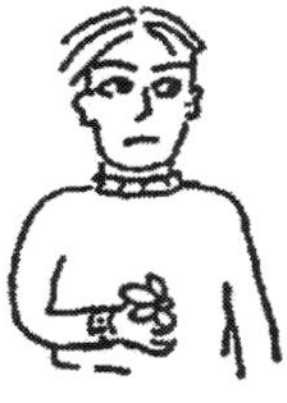

SHE'S WATCHING ME...
SHE'S WATCHING ME NOT.

ANTISOCIAL

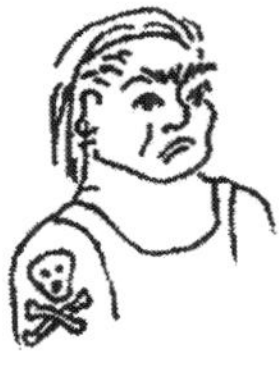

I DON'T GIVE A DAMN
IF SHE LOVES ME OR NOT.

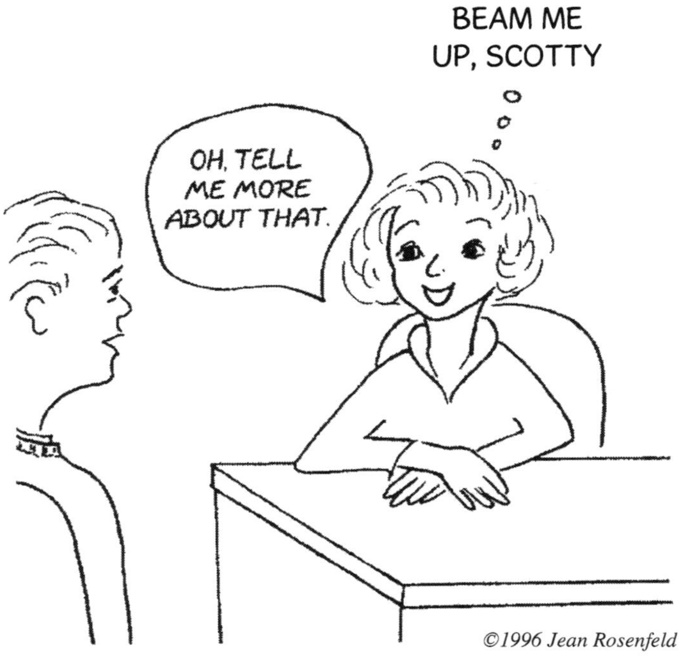
BEAM ME
UP, SCOTTY
OH, TELL
ME MORE
ABOUT THAT.
©1996 Jean Rosenfeld

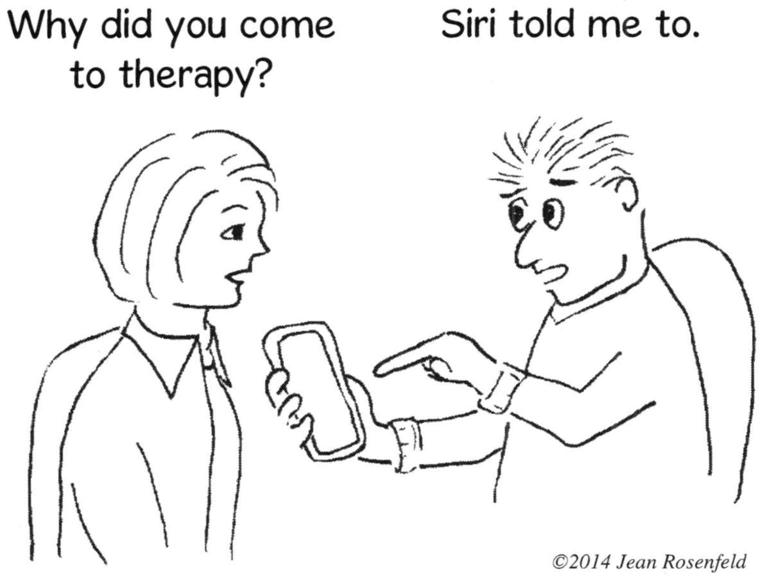
Why did you come to therapy?
Siri told me to.
©2014 Jean Rosenfeld

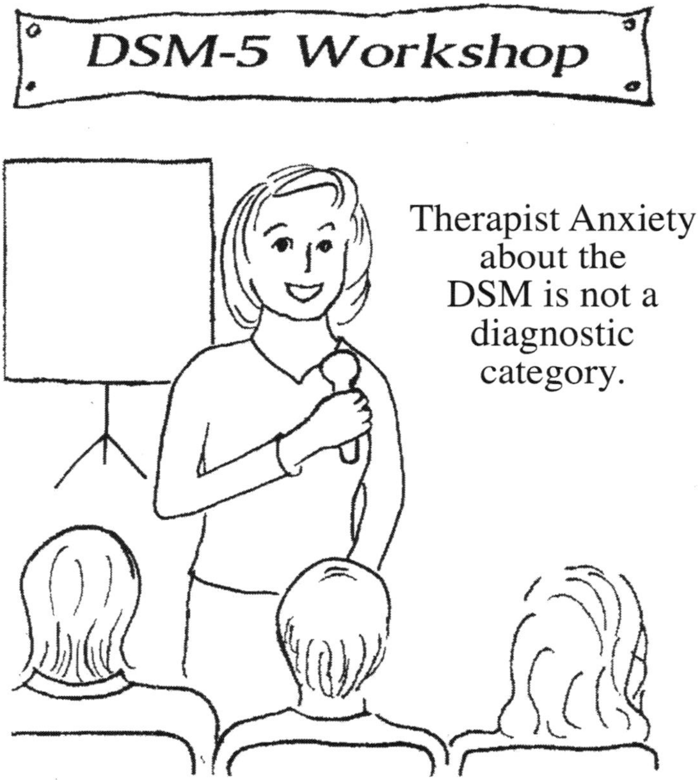
DSM-5 Workshop
Therapist Anxiety about the DSM is not a diagnostic category.

©2014 Jean Rosenfeld

Losing clients to personal trainers?
Trade in your couch.

BOOKS
SELF-HELP FOR THERAPIST BURNOUT
SELF-HURT
Feigning Empathy
The 15 Minute Hour
1,000 Ways to Say Unh-huh
Therapist Centered Therapy
Passive Listening
Visualize Cancellations
50 Ways to Stifle Yawns

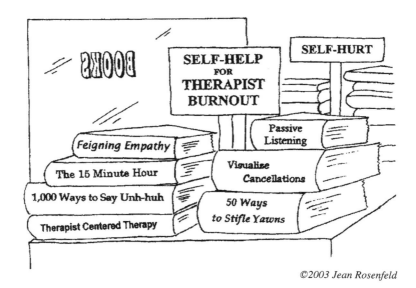

©2003 Jean Rosenfeld

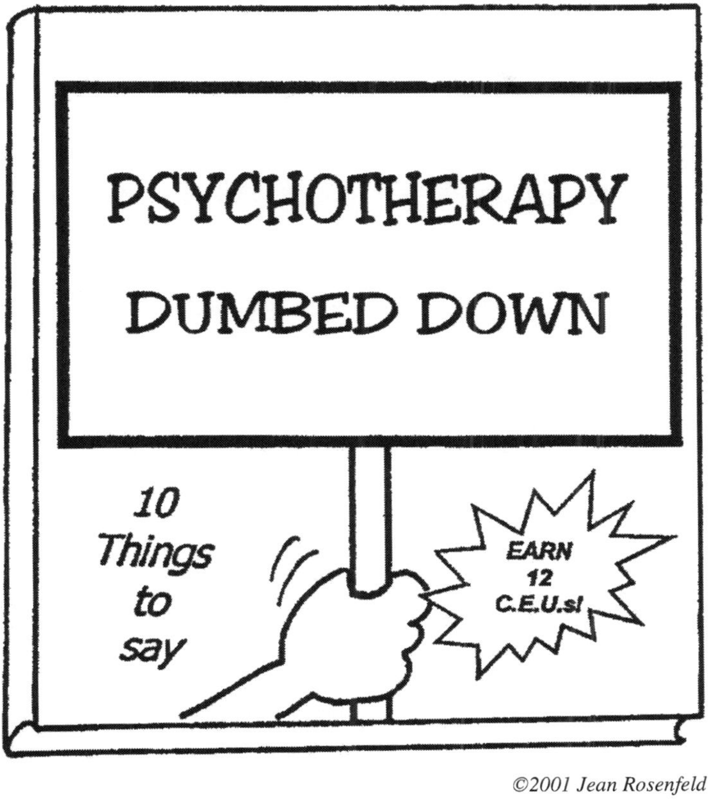
PSYCHOTHERAPY
DUMBED DOWN
10
Things
to
say
EARN
12
C.E.U.s!

©2011 Jean Rosenfeld

Would medication help or hurt?

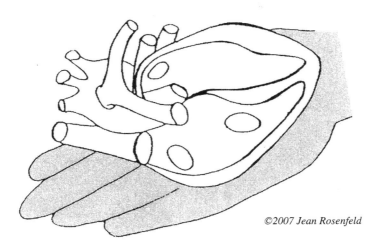

©2007 Jean Rosenfeld

Sometimes gifts from clients
can be challenging.

YES, I DO TREAT PEOPLE WITH COMPULSIVE SPENDING PROBLEMS. <u>NO!</u> YOU MAY NOT PAY BY **CREDIT CARD!**

©1999 Jean Rosenfeld

Daydreams of a Therapist:
What I would do if I had no boundaries and some random magical powers...

- I'd tell the parents of the college student that he drinks, drugs and lies
- I'd go to the bipolar alcoholic's house and pour his vodka down the drain.
- I'd flirt with the jazz piano playing philosophy professor.
- I'd give some marijuana to the uptight math teacher.
- I'd fix up the adorable-but-shy welfare worker with the oh-so-earnest environmentalist.
- I'd tell the depressed, well-dressed-obsessed party girl that she is shallow as a puddle.
- I'd tell the wealthy, severely right-wing CEO that he is thick as a brick; then I'd give him an identity transplant.
- I'd hire a personal shopper for the aging diva whose necklines plunge too low.
- I'd give the over-confidant, fundamentalist preacher a bad case of existential doubt and fear.

And I'd hand out as needed: brains, hearts, courage, good health, common sense, self-confidence, financial security, hopefulness and some really good chocolate.

©2016 Jean Rosenfeld

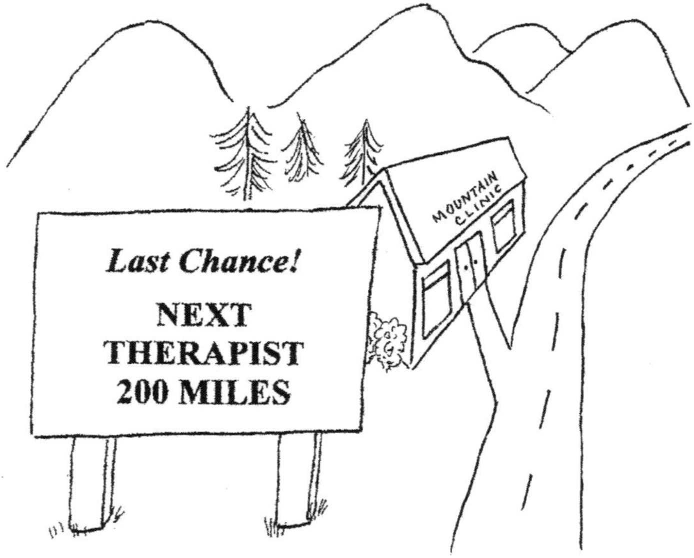
MOUNTAIN CLINIC
Last Chance!
NEXT
THERAPIST
200 MILES

©1996 Jean Rosenfeld

Animals

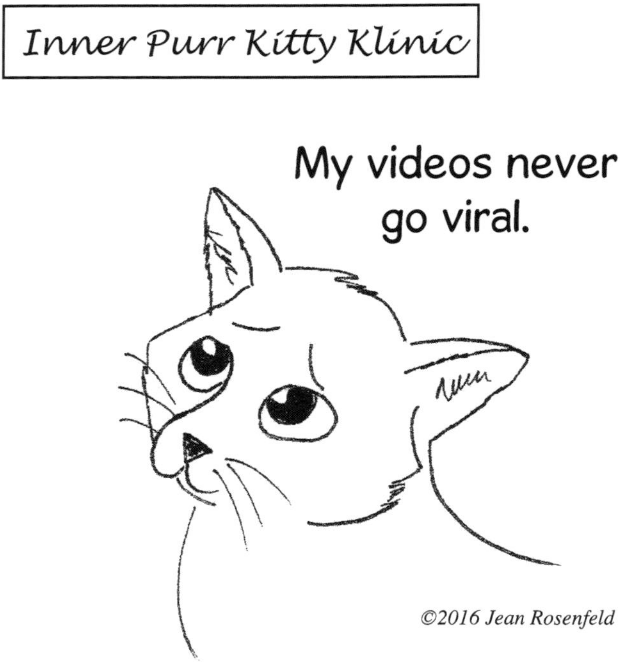
Inner Purr Kitty Klinic
My videos never go viral.
©2016 Jean Rosenfeld

I'm Polar—not Bipolar!

©2015 Jean Rosenfeld

I'm the one everyone
ignores in the room.

©2014 Jean Rosenfeld

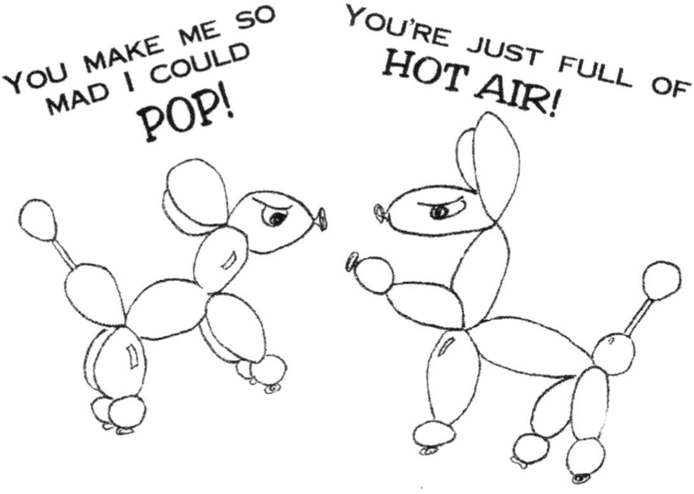
YOU MAKE ME SO MAD I COULD POP!
YOU'RE JUST FULL OF HOT AIR!
©2012 Jean Rosenfeld

THESE PROBLEMS MAY
BALLOON OUT OF CONTROL

FLY TRAUMA CENTER

©2016 Jean Rosenfeld

"I was caught in a NO FLY zone!
And then the SWAT TEAM arrived
and I barely escaped with my life!"

ABOUT THE CARTOONIST

 Jean Rosenfeld has been a Licensed Clinical Social Worker in private practice in the Sacramento area for over 30 years with a mission to help people live more fulfilling lives. She treats individuals and couples in short- and long-term psychotherapy using a variety of modalities. At Sacramento Children's Home she worked with teens and their families, and provided consultation to the social work team.

Throughout her career she has helped to provide clinical education as well as community building among therapists primarily through her involvement in the California Society for Clinical Social Work (clinicalsocialworksociety. org) and Therapists for Social Responsibility (therapistsforsocialresponsibility.org).

She and her husband, George Rosenfeld, created The Pregnancy Game that was used nationally in teen pregnancy programs to educate and encourage communication about pregnancy and parenthood. She illustrated and co-authored *Baby and Other Teachers* published by the Daycare and Child Development Council of America, and designed the testing board for the Child at Risk Screener published by McGraw Hill.

Jean says that "humor has been a mainstay of our family. Along with laughing at ourselves and the world, it has been present in numerous song parodies and silly poems to celebrate special occasions. It is no surprise that both our daughters married men with a good sense of humor and that our grandchildren are a riot!"

48424603R00059

Made in the USA
San Bernardino, CA
25 April 2017